T5-ANW-644

THE UNVEILING

AN OVERVIEW OF REVELATION

JACK HAYFORD

SCOTT BAUER • JACK HAMILTON

THE UNVEILING

A Practical, Introductory Guidebook for a Comprehensive Overview in the Bible Book of Revelation

Published by Living Way Ministries
14800 Sherman Way
Van Nuys, CA (USA) 91405-2499
(818) 779-8400 • (800) 776-8180

ISBN 0-916847-26-8
Printed in the United States of America.

TABLE OF CONTENTS

If this is your first use of the Bible Book-a-Month study guide, read pages 64-65.

REVELATION

KEY WORD:
"THE REVELATION
OF THE COMING OF CHRIST"

When the reader fully understands the end of history, the present is radically impacted. In Revelation 19–22 God's plans for the last days and for all eternity are recorded in explicit detail.

KEY CHAPTERS: REVELATION 19–22

KEY VERSES:

Write the things which you have seen, and the things which are, and the things which will take place after this.   Revelation 1:19

Now I saw heaven opened, and behold, a white horse. And He who sat on him was called Faithful and True, and in righteousness He judges and makes war.
                                        Revelation 19:11

Introducing the Bible Book of
REVELATION

Author:	John, the Apostle
Date:	A.D. 70 – 95
Theme:	The Lord Our God the Almighty Reigns
Key Words:	Throne, Lamb, Overcomes, Seven, I Saw

AUTHOR

Four times the author refers to himself as "John" (1:1, 4, 9; 22:8). He was so well known to his readers and his spiritual authority was so widely acknowledged that he did not need to establish his credentials. Early church tradition unanimously attributes this book to the apostle John.

DATE

Evidence within Revelation indicates that it was written during a period of extreme persecution of Christians, which possibly was that begun by Nero after the great fire that nearly destroyed Rome in July of A.D. 64 and continued until his suicide in June of A.D. 68. On the basis of isolated statements by the early church fathers, some interpreters date the book near the end of the reign of Domitian (A.D. 81–96), after John had fled to Ephesus.

PERIOD WHEN REVELATION WAS LIKELY WRITTEN

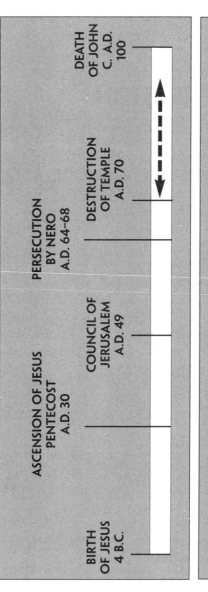

| BIRTH OF JESUS 4 B.C. | ASCENSION OF JESUS PENTECOST A.D. 30 | COUNCIL OF JERUSALEM A.D. 49 | PERSECUTION BY NERO A.D. 64–68 | DESTRUCTION OF TEMPLE A.D. 70 | DEATH OF JOHN C. A.D. 100 |

Revelation discloses the age-long struggle between good and evil and guarantees Christ's final triumph.

An Outline of
REVELATION

The Jesus of Revelation

words and music by Jack W. Hayford
June 18, 1989

To request a lead sheet of the song "The Jesus of Revelation"
send a self-addressed, stamped envelope to:
Living Way Ministries®
14820 Sherman Way, Van Nuys, CA 91405

THE SEVEN CHURCHES OF REVELATION

	COMMENDATION	CRITICISM	INSTRUCTION	PROMISE
EPHESUS (2:1–7)	Rejects evil, perseveres, has patience	Love for Christ no longer fervent	Do the works you did at first	The tree of life
SMYRNA (2:8–11)	Gracefully bears suffering	None	Be faithful until death	The crown of life
PERGAMOS (2:12–17)	Keeps the faith of Christ	Tolerates immorality, idolatry, and heresies	Repent	Hidden manna and a stone with a new name
THYATIRA (2:18–29)	Love, service, faith, patience is greater than at first	Tolerates cult of idolatry and immorality	Judgment coming; keep the faith	Rule over nations and receive morning star
SARDIS (3:1–6)	Some have kept the faith	A dead church	Repent; strengthen what remains	Faithful honored and clothed in white
PHILADELPHIA (3:7–13)	Perseveres in the faith	None	Keep the faith	A place in God's presence, a new name, and the New Jerusalem
LAODICEA (3:14–22)	None	Indifferent	Be zealous and repent	Share Christ's throne

Nelson's Complete Book of Maps and Charts © 1993, Thomas Nelson, Inc.

PART 1

THE PILLAR PRINCIPLES OF REVELATION

JACK HAYFORD

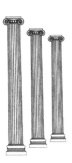

THE PILLAR PRINCIPLES OF
REVELATION

"The Unveiling," might well be a 2000 AD title for what continues to be, in every generation, the most fascinating book in the Bible—*Revelation!*

The Book of the Revelation of Jesus Christ, the real title of this prophetic masterpiece, captures our interest for many reasons:

- The imagery of the prophet attracts *curious* interest: a seven-headed beast, frog-like beings, earthquakes, and fire-from-heaven, are just samplings of the dramatic pictures.
- The message of hope threaded throughout the book brings a justifiable sigh of relief. As it has so often been said, "I've read the last page of the Book, *and we win!*"
- The recurrent message of the Second Coming of Jesus Christ, and the elements of the prophecy which seem to give time-signals warning us of both the nearness and the implications of His Coming, gains serious attention. And best of all,
- The glorious unveiling of *Jesus Himself*—seen in all His glory and power as The Lord of the Church, moving among the lampstands (a picture of His superintending presence), as He

15

administrates, admonishes, and leads us.

- These are *each one* sufficient to command our interest and stir our hearts with a quest to understand—to *grip* the message of promise, hope, and ultimate victory Revelation contains.

OUR GREATEST CHALLENGES

Without question, the greatest obstacle to our understanding Revelation is *not* the maze of events or the often bizarre images it contains. Instead, it is the *predisposition of mystery* and the *preoccupation with prophecy* which we too often bring to the Book; influenced, usually, by a prevailing mood conveyed by many teachers and found among most believers. Even the frequent use of the Greek name for this book, *Apocalypse,* has been made into a mysterious vision of end-times horrors of destruction and wrath. However, though these features are contained in Revelation, the meaning in the word (Gk. *apocalupsis*) is in fact the *opposite* of the mysterious and *doesn't* mean "destruction" or "horror." It is a word of expectancy and hope, and could even describe the beauty of a moment a bride's face is unveiled by her husband. So the heart of Revelation actually refers to "an unveiling"—a full disclosure of issues not seen or known until they are given.

To open Revelation and gain a real clarity of understanding, let me confront the two challenges that can easily blur the message which **Jesus** seems to be wanting to convey to His Church—*i.e., to you and me!* After all, we *are* His bride, and He wants us to both capture and be captivated by the promise of

His Coming, as well as the confidence of our future triumph with Him.

GAINING THE BIG PICTURE

Jesus is the central character of this book, even more than in the general sense that He is the central personality in *every* book of God's Word. Here, in Revelation, Jesus steps forward as the Redeemer— "the Lamb that was slain and the Lion of Judah who has prevailed" (5:6). To embrace the structure of the whole book, there are *three phrases* and *three phases* that provide us with a framework.

"Write the **things** which you **have seen**,
and the **things** which **are,**
and the **things** which **will take place**." (1:19)

Those three phrases <u>outline</u> Revelation. They relate to three phases of the Book's development:

Phase 1 (Chapter 1): Jesus' visitation to John on Patmos is the introduction of Revelation. It is more than a historic narrative; it reveals the way Jesus comes to meet with and care for His own when they are enduring long-term difficulty.

Phase 2 (Chapters 2, 3): Jesus' directive to John, to write His words to "the seven churches in Asia" (1:11) is a description of more than the individual condition of the churches mentioned. It is a summary analysis of those victories and problems— the upside and the downside of the Church *everywhere in every age.* Issues here are relevant to today —not just the past. The life and spiritual well-being of the Church is in focus, and sensitive believers and leaders will give attention. Chapters 2 and 3 set forward the *ever-present call to the Church*—**remember,**

repent, and *overcome!*

Phase 3 (Chapters 4–22): Jesus' post-resurrection appearance at the Throne of God the Father (chap. 4, 5) begins His message of *things that will take place.* From chapter 6 to the end of Revelation, "The Unveiling" takes place—but always remember: It is JESUS' *Lordship, Dominion, and Triumph* that are the focus. The striking images, the horrifying judgments, the terrifying warfare—these are real and not to be unnoticed. But they are **not** the point of this Book. **JESUS' VICTORY IS!** Keep that in mind to keep a clear focus on the Revelation.

Revelation's
CENTRAL PERSONALITIES

1. Jesus Christ. The Savior's appearance to John, who has been exiled to the Isle of Patmos, is the foremost character in this Book. He is both the fountainhead of the Book's contents (1:8, 17–20), and the focus of the Book's finale (19:11–16; 21:5–6; 22:1, 7, 12, 16).

2. John, often called "the beloved"; the last one of the 12 apostles still living at the time; the brother of James and writer of the Gospel and Epistles of John. He appears throughout, reporting the visions Jesus is unveiling to Him.

3. Angels. Though the first mention of "angel" in this book is not to a heavenly being, after chapters 2, 3 (where the "*messenger*" [angelos] role of the local pastor is referenced) angelic creatures are greatly involved. All the angels mentioned are shown as united in worship and in service as divinely assigned emissaries. They are active instruments in the fulfilling of God's will on earth in response to (a) His heavenly plan and purpose as, (b) it is loosed on earth by the prayers of His people.

AS TO OTHERS…A bevy of other personalities or groups appear, such as the 144,000 (7:4–8; 14:1–5); the Two Witnesses (11:1–13); the Beast and the False Prophet (13:1–18); and the great harlot (17–18), but none command as central a role as the above.

Key Concepts of
REVELATION

The Book of Revelation may be summarized by noting twelve pillar truths it reveals.

1. The Majesty of the Lord Jesus.
John's last encounter with the visible Savior was probably a half century before. Suddenly, a trumpet-like voice sounds and he turns to witness his Lord at a new dimension. Chapter 1:9–20 gives a detailed description of the radiant beauty of our Ascended Lord. Each feature of His appearance reveals a trait of His Person; traits that are significant to the letters He dictates to John to be written to His Church.

Chapters 2, 3 contain *The Epistles of Jesus Christ.* The seven letters reveal three things:

(1) Foremost, is the presence, discernment, and commanding concern of our Lord for His Church. He has not "left," though He is away, and He is actively *present*—always (e.g 2:1).

(2) Secondly, Jesus both graciously and demandingly confronts His own with their good works as well as their bad. He *discerns* between these in a way pointing to practical solutions (e.g. 2:2–6).

(3) Finally, there is a consistent balance applying His lordly role—He commands repentance, and He offers the promises of the overcomers blessings to those who respond (e.g. 2:5, 7).

2. The Magnificence of the Lamb.

Chapters 4, 5 unveil the scene of transcendent splendor around the Throne of God. Suddenly, an appearance is made by one described as "a Lamb as though it had been slain" (literally, "a lamb with the marks of having been slaughtered.)

Ironically, this Lamb is introduced as a Lion—a paradox in terms, but an accurate description: the Lord has triumphed in battle, but at the cost of His sacrifice.

From this introductory vision of the Lamb, Jesus is referenced by that term 25 times in 11 chapters of this Book. It is apparent that this is His title of honor—that though He is King of kings and Lord of lords (19:16), the Alpha and Omega (1:8, 11; 21:6; 22:13), the Root and the Offspring of David, the Bright and Morning Star (22:16); the Faithful Witness and the Firstborn from the Dead (1:5), the Almighty (1:8) and the Amen (3:14)—Jesus' title of preference is "the Lamb."

This provides us with a commentary on the heart of God and His ways. His "heart" is always disposed toward *the redemptive* and to *the restorative* —to save and to serve. As the Lamb, Jesus came to *seek and to save*; to rescue at the price of His death, and to restore by the power of His life. This is why throughout the ages to come we will find ourselves overawed and constantly worshipping Him as the Lamb—"who loved us and washed us from our sins in His own blood" (1:5; 5:9, 12–13).

3.   The Scroll Received by the Lamb.

The centerpiece of the Book of Revelation is a Scroll in the hand of the Almighty Father (5:1). As that chapter describes it, Jesus Christ is given an authority earned by reason of His death and resurrection—the right to take and open the Scroll. Virtually everything that follows in the entirety of the Book distills from this "opening."

Nothing is more basic to our understanding all of Revelation than capturing a sense of what this Scroll represents. We can grasp its significance when we simply look at the fact: *as soon as this Scroll is fully unsealed and opened, earth is restored under the rule of God and His Christ.* It thus becomes apparent that the Scroll represents <u>The Title Deed to Planet Earth</u>. The domain once given to man (Genesis 1:26, 28; Psalm 115:16), through his fall became the domain of satanic darkness (1 John 5:19; John 14:30). However, the Lamb has broken the power of evil's rule (1 John 3:8; Colossians 2:14–15), and is *now in process* of driving out the oppressive works of hell through His Church at war under His leadership (Revelation 12:7–12).

This helps define the nature of Revelation's judgments, which are for the most part *God's means of ridding the earth of evil*—i.e., "delivering" Earth; reclaiming its terrain as a place of His originally intended purposes. The Scroll's un*seal*ing results in the *trumpets* and *bowls*—all of which converge in an eventual new heaven and new earth. Revelation is the narration of this struggle-unto-deliverance from heaven's perspective.

4.   The Praise and Prayer of the Saints.

The primary instruments of the Church in conducting its age-long warfare as a part of this "struggle" is in the spirit of dynamic, Christ-exalting worship. Chapter 5:8 describes "the prayers of the saints" as a present, cumulative "fund" of intercession maintained in heaven, *then*…. The next thing that unfolds is a description of *how* those "prayers" are expressed: praiseful song and glorious worship seem to explode around the Throne of God (v.9, 12–13).

This is all the more significant when it is seen in the larger context of the whole of Revelation. It seems more than coincidental that praise and worship *precede* each major step in the unfolding of the Scroll. In short, *the process of Christ's achieving the RELEASE of His purpose is linked directly to the prayers of His people. (*NOTE: A study of the chart on the next page displays this concept.)

5.   The Discursive Nature of The Prophecy.

A fundamental point in studying the prophetic literature of the Bible is to remember that the

Ch. 4, 5	_precedes_	Ch. 6
Worship at the Throne…		**Opening of Seals**
Ch. 7:9–17; 8:1–5	_precedes_	Ch. 8:6–9:21
Prayers and worship…		**Sounding of Trumpets**
Ch. 15:1–8	precedes	Ch. 16–18
The worshipping throng…		**Pouring out of Vials**

prophets _see_ things shown or spoken to them by the Spirit of God, but they do not know any more about the timing of the prophecy or the order in which its parts may be fulfilled. _Time and sequence_ are always uncertain from our point of view, because they were unknown to the prophet's under-standing—_unless specifically stated_. (Example: Jeremiah 25:11–12, the prophet declares God's announced _seventy year_ judgment on the exiles. However, in that text as in most, the beginning date from which the measurement starts is not clearly understood until _after_ its fulfillment.)

John, like most all Bible prophets, relates the future, but in recording his visions gives us virtually no definition of time. Perhaps no phrase in the Bible has been more misapplied than John's "after these things." (4:1; 7:1; 7:9; 15:5; 18:1; 19:1). To protect against presumption in study, and to keep from creating presumed time structures which cre-ate _charted systems_ of supposed certainty in sequence, it is essential to remember the *discursive* nature of prophecy. <u>This refers to the method in which the prophet relates what he sees, ranging from one topic to another without any particular regard for synchronizing time or order.</u>

We must emphasize this principle strongly. The thought-habits of many have long led them to interpret Revelation without consideration for this principle. By reinforcing it, we avoid being trapped in systems of human prediction, and find a *release of the whole of Revelation's practical, as well as prophetic truth*:

From presumed structures that restrict the broader application of the Book to *all* of the believer's life *today* as well as future; and,

From a "sequential" approach to the central prophetic picture-message of the Book—the unfolding of the Seals, Trumpets, and Bowls.

6. The Overlap and Interweave of Events.

It is the above *discursive* form of Revelation that helps us grasp the *Scroll's* "unveiling," as the Seven Seals, Trumpets, and Bowls then become viewed as overlapping and interweaving, rather than necessarily in a regimented sequence; whereby each is required to following in order, rather than be seen as a succession of judgments, but not necessarily always in sequential order. (See the chart on the adjacent page.)

7. The Avoidance of the Distractive.

All scripture is intended to edify the believer, and the "unveiling" called the Book of Revelation is

THE UNLEASHING OF THE IMPLICATIONS OF THE SCROLL'S UNFOLDING
The Path and the Price of Evil's Overthrow and the Son of Man's Restored Rule

The "core" of the events constituting Revelation is in the three sets of sevens—the *seals*, *trumpets*, and *bowls*. Our approach to this study does not interpret these as historically sequential—i.e., following one another. Rather, they are seen as integrated and overlapping, except for those events which are defined as "God's wrath."

SEALS Ch. 6   These seem to be AGE-LONG, as with Jesus' prophecies, and essentially involve *Man's Actions.*

30 A.D.   Comprehensive (Throughout)   **(*) The End**

TRUMPETS Ch. 8 & 9   These seem to be PROPORTIONS of destructiveness cumulative through the age, and essentially involve demonic action. (See also Revelation 11:15–19.)

30 A.D.   Controlled (Increasing Intensity)   **(*) The End**

BOWLS Ch. 16   These are clearly CLIMACTIC outpourings of His final "wrath," and essentially involve *God's action.*

            Cumulative (Begins in Last Times)   **(*) ▶ (**) The End**

*The common denominator or coordinating factors regarding "The End" are earthquakes ("an earthquake" or "a great earthquake"—Revelation 6:12; 11:13; 16:18). There seems to be two: one (*) at the beginning of God's wrath outpoured (6:12) which is the probable time of the rapture of the Church (1 Thessalonians 1:10; 5:9); and the second (**) at the conclusion of this display of wrath in judgment (16:18); and the second (**) at the conclusion of this display of wrath in judgment (16:18). Some feel the 7th Trumpet is the same as "the last trump." (See 1 Corinthians 15:52 and 1 Thessalonians 4:16.)

25

certainly not intended to mystify. For that reason, I have concluded, *if a feature of Revelation seems puzzling, avoid becoming distracted to the point of pursuing curiosity or speculation.*

Three cases provide the primary points for applying this principle; the three "parties" which have constantly bred inquiry and guesswork:

Who are the 144,000? (I hold that this is a symbolic number, but who can say for sure?)

Who are the Two Witnesses? (Chapter 11 is, to my view, the hardest in the Book.)

Who are the beings called the Beast "from the sea" and "from the earth"? (13:1, 11).

There has unquestionably been more labeling of individuals or groups as a result of "prophetic study" than any other guessing enterprise in Church history. My conviction is that we are wisest to capture the practical principles revealed in regard to these personalities, then leave them alone. Speculation, no matter how much fun, is never edifying, and it holds the danger of drawing us away—distracting us from the purpose of this Book.

8. The Place of the Timelessly Chosen.

There is no way to escape the obvious fact that Revelation is a book with the Jewish peoples in mind. Of course, the *Revelation is for us all,* but there are distinct signals within the Book which focus God's timeless commitment to His ancient and chosen people.

The frequent references to the heavenly "court and temple" (3:12; 7:15; 11:1–2, 19; 14:15, 17; 15:5–8; 16:1, 17) draw us to the *roots* of God's redemptive plan. The very style of such writing is an integrative means of drawing two things into perspective: (1) the place of the Old Covenant as it supports the New (Romans 11:16–22); (2) the intent of God to fulfill His timeless purpose among His chosen, as a part of completing the entirety of His purpose for mankind.

The words of Revelation 11:2, regarding the "court" reserved for the Gentiles, should be seen in the dramatic link Jesus' reference makes there to His own words in Luke 21:24, and the mention of "the fullness of the Gentiles" in Romans 11:25. These three texts tie together "the very end of time" with two things: (a) the conclusion of the Gentile age—often called, the Age of Grace; and (b) a climactic last-days ingathering of Jews to their Messiah, Jesus.

9. The World's Transiency and Impurity.

Revelation contains many soul-wrenching, fear-inspiring scenes, but probably the most poignant is the devastating cry that is emitted by "the kings of the earth" in Revelation 16:16— **"Alas, alas…*in one hour such great riches came to nothing!"*** These who cry out are the merchants of the earth who trafficked in the most commercially valuable and the most corruptingly vile—taking all that is precious (including "the souls of men") and cheapening it for whatever gain may be gotten (see Revelation 17:1–4; 18:3–13). But suddenly—it is all gone!

What a strong reminder that heaven's call to holiness is not merely a call from what cheapens life and destroys souls. It is also a sober warning that affirms the transiency if all this world holds valuable: it counts for so little now, and in the end it will count for nothing.

10. The Ultimate Triumph of Christ's Own.

The Chapter 1 encounter between John and Jesus which opens this Book, sets the tone and the target for its being written. *The primary message of Revelation's prophecy is not the horror of the world's impending judgment, but the glory of Christ's people ultimate triumph!*

Keep this in view when reading Revelation. The messages to the seven churches (Revelation 2, 3) constantly set forth the high promise and reward of "overcoming" faith.

- Recurrent exhortations to patience and comfort amid trial are present (Revelation 13:10; 14:12).
- Assurance of victories in the battles spiritual warfare engages is given (Revelation 12:10–11).
- A clear message of ultimate comfort and reward are sewn through the fabric of the Book (Revelation 7:13–17; 15:1–5).

Finally, the Bride is seen: (a) joined to the Lamb, Her heavenly husband (19:1–9); (b) moving with Him into the climactic battle of the ages (19:11–21); and with Him forever in the New Jerusalem and before God's Throne (21:1–7; 22:1–5).

11. The Imminency of Christ's Coming.

One of the greatest values of regularly reading of the Book of Revelation is that it softens the heart and keeps the soul from becoming calloused against *a tender, ready expectancy* concerning Jesus' Second Coming.

Time passes. We are all too vulnerable to the jading influence of the world, not to mention the ease with which the spiritually informed soul may become presumptuous or passive on this issue.

"***Behold, I am coming quickly!***" Chapter 22 resounds with a *triple trumpet call to the soul* (vs. 7, 12, 20.) This reveals the heartbeat of Jesus Himself toward us: He wants us to live in constant expectancy; not as a "tease," but as a "trust." The Bride who "loves His appearing," will maintain a love for HIM!

12. The Church's Path to Triumph *NOW!*

Revelation most touches each of us when we see the end-times vision clearly from its initial point of reference: Jesus, walking among the churches… standing in our midst…present *now* as our Savior, Lord, and Coming King (2:1; 1:12; 3:20). He is with us in trial to bring assurance (1:12); walking in our midst, reviewing what we are and what we do (2:1); and calling us to open to Him at new dimensions (3:20).

His recurring call to repentance is not so much a condemning or haranguing word of criticism as it is a call to victory. OVERCOME! That's His call, His hope for us, and within each "overcome" is the highest of promise and the fullest of hope.

This is Revelation: CHRIST HIMSELF— coming NOW to protect and equip us for victory in life's struggles, warfare, and persecution; and coming AGAIN to be united with His Church—His beloved one: you and me!

THE SEVEN
CHURCHES

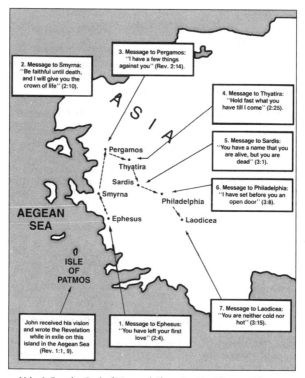

Nelson's Complete Book of Maps and Charts © 1993, Thomas Nelson, Inc.

PART 2

THE RELEVANT ANSWERS IN REVELATION

SCOTT BAUER

Questions in
REVELATION

The book of Revelation is the most complex and difficult book to interpret in the Bible. It has spawned endless speculations that have brought about some of the divisions we see in the Body of Christ today. It has become a matter of dogmas that divide, as some confidently assert to an absolute knowledge of this book and its secrets. However, the book of Revelation demands to be treated with respect because, in its reading and our faithful response, there is a blessing (1:3). But there is also a curse to those who embellish or diminish its words (22:18–19). It is a matter of utmost importance to God that believers read and respond to this book of prophecy. As we seek to understand God's heart and purpose in providing us insight into the last days, we ought to accept a place of humility, knowing that at best we "know in part and we prophesy in part" (1 Corinthians 13:9). As this applies to the Word of God, it is, indeed, complete. However, as it relates to our understanding of that complete Word, we must link our opinions and interpretations with a thorough commitment to our brotherhood in the Body of Christ which unites us. And we must come with humility which allows the Lord God of Heaven to surprise us as His tomorrows unfold in our experience.

The approach to interpreting this book must be clearly defined. There are some who adhere to a strict, literal interpretation of the text of Revelation. However, in accepting this perspective in approaching the book, virtually all commentators acknowledge the limitation of language and experience of John to describe what he witnessed in the Revelation as given him by Jesus. The mere mention of locusts (chapter nine) with men's faces, women's hair, iron breastplates, sounds of chariots, and stinging tails, does describe what was seen, but its translation in a literal sense defies our complete understanding. In much of the book, future events are descriptive and literal in the sense of their being real—but when applied to technologies and culture thousands of years later, it adds a speculative quality to even the most faithful attempts of literalism in interpretation. Others have tried to relegate this book to the realm of spiritual allegory where the vision itself is simply representative of a spiritual likeness which can only be loosely applied in its absolute form. When it is applied in its allegorical (rather than literal) sense, the fulfillment of prophecy is deemed to have occurred at various times and seasons in the life of the Church.

For most serious scholars who are committed to a view of Scripture which demands a more literal approach to the text, the notion of Revelation as allegory is an unsettling one. However, two things are true about this book. First, it does describe the actual events of the end of the world. Second, it does offer a view into the heavenly realm which applies to the Church in every generation—not just the final one. The struggle of Satan against God is not new. Neither is it confined to only the last moments of history. The truths revealed in Revelation have points of application to every generation. The speculative nature of most interpretations of this book often prevent these prevailing truths from being explored, because the fascination of personalities, timelines, and current events obscure the broader message of Christ to His Church.

The Body of Christ is to be prepared for His Second Coming. In the meantime, there is a struggle for the advancing of the Kingdom of God on earth. As the Church, we can expect severe spiritual resistance to the advance of His Kingdom culminating, one day, in the events described in this book. However, Revelation is not merely a futuristic rendering of events yet to transpire. It is a message to the Church about the nature of the opposition we face in our world, the need to **prepare** ourselves for His coming, and why we must deepen our commitment to **persuade** others to do the same (2 Timothy 4:1–5).

The greatest points of question and speculation in this book relate to: a) time—when will these things happen; b) personalities—who are the individuals and peoples described in the text; and c) the events—what is going to happen in the various scenes described in the Revelation? The exact interpretation of the who, what, and when has served to excite the Church throughout the ages—and also, it tended to distract from the broader issues of personal preparedness and the advance of the Gospel to those who have yet to hear it. Therefore, as we seek to answer some of the more interesting questions in Revelation, it is vital to understand that the primary focus of the book is on Christ's coming to establish His eternal Kingdom and the cleansing of our world from the final ravages of sin and disobedience.

THE "WHOS" OF
REVELATION

The most asked questions concerning the people of Revelation are centered in three general questions. First, who are the one hundred and forty-four thousand of Revelation 7:4 and 14:1, 3? The question revolves around the unique relationship they have to the Lord in the last times. There are groups who seek to assert their peculiar standing before God by identifying with this group. Second, who are the two witnesses described in Revelation 11:10 and what is their purpose in the end-time's revival? Third, who are the beast and the false prophet of Revelation 13? Though the name "Antichrist" is not found in Revelation, there appears to be a correlation in concept with the personalities of evil as seen in the beast and the false prophet. The examination of these identities leads us to establish a context for those who serve God and advance His Kingdom during the end-times and those who oppose God and seek to persecute believers and thwart the work of God in delivering the planet from the powers of evil.

Once again, it needs to be understood that the various interpretive schemes and our perspective on the Bible itself dramatically impact the kinds of conclusions which arise over a study of the people of Revelation. Given those differing perspectives, there is little possibility that the whole Body of Christ will agree on the conclusions reached by any single interpreter. However, in its broadest understandings, there is much to be gained in studying these individuals.

The problems arise when the types and generalities which apply to the personalities of Revelation become fixed in personalities found in the current events of the times. The need of some segments of the Body of Christ to "know," fuels fruitless attempts to alert the Church to current dangers and individuals which pose a threat to the people of God. The problem with that kind activity is obvious. It can tend to be politically motivated (particularly if the interpreter is attempting to vilify the person), or it can serve to emphasize exclusivity (especially as it relates one group's superiority over any other). Therefore, great discernment needs to be exercised as we consider the "Whos" of Revelation.

Who Are the 144,000? (Revelation 7:4)

The majority of commentators see the 144,000 as representing the Church of Jesus Christ that has come through the tumultuous end of the Age. The reason for this is found in Revelation 7:9–17. The relationship between the 144,000 and the "great multitude which no one could number, of all nations, tribes, peoples, and tongues" has been made. The presumption is that a literal interpretation of the 144,000 seems quite unlikely and that it is to be understood in its symbolic reference to those who live in covenantal relationship with God based on the New Covenant found in Christ.

There is, however, one discomforting dimension to this interpretation of the 144,000—"These are the ones who come out of the great tribulation, and washed their robes and made them white in the blood of the Lamb" (7:14); "And God will wipe away every tear" (7:17). By identifying this group with the Church, there seems to be an inescapable relationship between them and suffering in the great tribulation.

One of the principle doctrines of much of the evangelical Church in the past century has been that the true Church will escape persecution in a "pre-tribulation rapture." This text directly challenges this notion if the Church is identified with the 144,000. Clearly, the action of sealing "the servants of our God on their foreheads" (7:3) refers to the Holy Spirit's ability to keep His people faithful in the midst of the most intense pressures and persecutions.

The absolute identification of the 144,000 with the Church creates another kind of tension on the scriptures. Obviously, John, in recording what He is seeing, knows the difference between the diverse multitude found in 7:9 and Israel. He is not unclear about the fact that these are the tribes of Israel. "One hundred and forty-four thousand of all the tribes of the children of Israel were sealed" (7:4). This is clearly different from what is recorded in 7:9. John understood these 144,000 to be Jews. In order to find a different understanding from the obvious intent of John's words, we must place this passage within the context of an interpretive scheme which by-passes the most literal interpretation of the passage.

Romans 11:26–36 is exceedingly specific about the future of Israel—"so all Israel will be saved, as it is written" (v.26). The clear understanding of Romans 11 refers to the Jews. This has perplexed some Bible interpreters who have then sought to interpret Romans 11 as referring to the Church. The spiritualizing of the text can then be applied in Revelation 7 to the 144,000. However, that is not the most obvious rendering of the text in either case. And in fact, the 144,000 found in Revelation 7 may be a fulfillment of what is declared in Romans 11 where it affirms "all Israel will be saved."

If Revelation 7:4 does refer to Israel, then we have every right to expect that in the last days many Jews will turn to Jesus as their Messiah and Savior. It is unlikely that they will be identified as "Christians" in the conventional sense, but will retain their rightful identity as Jews who have been "completed" in their understanding the Messiah of Judaism.

Who Are the Two Witnesses? (Revelation 11:3)

The text suggests that the two witnesses are individuals. They are described as "two olive trees and the two lampstands" (11:4). The olive trees represent Holy Spirit-fullness and supernatural power to witness. The lampstands represent the witness of the Church bearing the light in a dark world (Revelation 1:12).

These witnesses possess supernatural powers to accomplish their task (11:6), they are martyred (11:7), and the world celebrates their death (11:10) because their witness, which has tormented the earth, is brought to an end. Their martyred bodies are found in the street (11:8), and they are resurrected and ascend to heaven in full of view of the unbelieving world (11:11–12). Some have believed that these witnesses are actually two individuals whose supernatural end-time's witness is a miraculous sign for the whole world to repent—in anticipation of the return of the Lord.

Other scholars believe that the witnesses of chapter 11 are, in fact, the Church in action. The concept of two witnesses is essential in the legal process as described by the Law (Deuteronomy 17:6) and from the words of Jesus (John 5:31–32). This dual witness confirms its veracity and demands a response of repentance from the watching world. From this perspective, the Body of Christ is overcome (v.8) by an Antichrist world system—"Egypt," and by a corrupted religious system—"Sodom," and all this will be centered in the place of Christ's death —Jerusalem.

The point of the passage is clear—there will be dynamic supernatural witness to the world in the last days. The world will not be able to resist the Truth without rejecting the verification of the miraculous testimony of the two witnesses. The world will be held accountable for rejecting this clear proclamation of Truth.

Who Are the Beast and the False Prophet? (Revelation 19:20)

One thing is absolutely certain, this beast is thoroughly satanic. In 13:1 it is described as having seven heads and ten horns and each of the horns has a crown and it rises out of the sea. The prophecy of Daniel contains a similar composite picture which we know shows the political dominance of various kingdoms throughout history. The same is true here. The beast represents political power—horns with crowns. And this power was given to the beast from "the dragon" (13:2), another name for the devil.

It is clear that its seven heads have no crowns. In Scripture, the head always refers to authority, not just power. However, this beast is able "to make war with the saints and to overcome them" (13:7). The power of this beast is worldwide.

Another beast rises from the earth in 13:11. Later, this one is identified as the false prophet in 16:13. This beast has supernatural powers and "deceives those who dwell on the earth" (13:14). There is also an absolute authority over the economic systems of the world related to this beast (13:16–18), represented by the "666" found in 13:18.

The beast relates to the "great harlot" in 17:7. This harlot is the focus of all idolatry on the planet. Once again, speculation concerning the identification of this "person" in Revelation tends to breed a response based in spiritual prejudices and rivalries. Each group lays claim to their own spiritual superiority while vilifying those who disagree. The speculations are endless, but they all avoid the most obvious conclusions.

The questions concerning the personalities of the beast and the false prophet/Antichrist, have caused many to focus on a second-guessing of who these individuals might be. Clearly, the issue of scripture places no importance on this whatsoever. "Experts" have conjectured for centuries over who it might be. And in succeeding generations, they have all proven to be wrong. However, the spirit of resistance to God and His way has always been with us. The Antichrist spirit that we are warned of in 1 John 4:3 "is now already in the world." We search for personalities when the more important matter of the spirit of Antichrist is constantly at work in our world.

Matthew 24:24 warns of "false christs and false prophets." The context is the end-times—but this injunction has always had a relevance to every segment of Church history. The devil's war against God and His people has never ceased. It is only the vigilant prayer in the power of the Holy Spirit and close communion with the Savior which insulates His people from the deceptive works of darkness in any age.

The "Whats" of
REVELATION

The book of Revelation offers insight into many interesting truths in Scripture which then opens the imagination to all kinds of possibilities. What is Heaven? We all have preconceptions because of artists' depictions and cultural notions—but what does the Bible say about Heaven? What will happen at the Judgment? Almost every person suffers some sort of anguish over the very thought of the Judgment—how does God intend to exercise ultimate justice regarding the things of earth? Also, what does the Bible teach about the Millennium? We hear about it, but where is it in the Bible?

What Does the Bible Say About Heaven?

"And I heard a loud voice from heaven saying, 'Behold, the tabernacle of God is with men, and He will dwell with them, and they shall be His people, and God Himself will be with them and be their God'" (Revelation 21:3). The Bible also describes heaven as being the place of ultimate consolation, comfort, and peace. Tears will be wiped away, and God will personally attend to each of His own— "I will be his God, and he shall be My son" (21:7).

Heaven has no temple in it. There is no need for a sun or moon, and there is no night. And nothing shall defile it. The glory of God will be the light, and His divine protection means that people will no longer fear things which might hurt them. Heaven is the dwelling place of God and His people—it is our eternal destination. But beyond the description of Chapter 21, the only things we know about Heaven are speculative. However, we do know this—Jesus has gone to prepare a place for each of us (John 14:2–3). There is only one thing left to know about Heaven that is of ultimate importance—only those whose names are written in the Lamb's Book of Life may enter (21:27). This is not a matter of exclusivity; it is a matter of faith.

Heaven has no restrictions of the kinds of people who may enter—but one thing is certain, the only doorway to eternity is the same for everyone. The rich cannot buy their way through the door; the good cannot do enough to merit their entrance; the poor cannot be forbidden to enter. And the most vile among us may enter the same way everyone else does—through Jesus. He said—"I am the door. If anyone enters by Me, he will be saved" (John 10:9). Faith in Jesus Christ places every person on equal footing before God. All are offered a second chance, and no one has a headstart. Faith demands all that we have—and that is all that we need. Ephesians 2:8 declares faith to be a gift from God—the same gift given to every person so that all might come to know the blessings of eternal life with God.

What About Judgment?

The Bible is clear that all will be judged (Revelation 20:12). The works of each will be reviewed from the "books." However, for those whose names are recorded in the Book of Life, they escape the eternal punishment which is described as the "lake of fire."

Many people refuse to acknowledge the possibility that a loving God would condemn people to eternal torment. They teach in error that God will ultimately reconcile all things to Himself. This is not taught in Scripture. In fact, 2 Peter 3:10 describes the burning up of all things which are present on the earth. And 2 Thessalonians 1:8–9 insists that God will be "taking vengeance on those who do not know God, and on those who do not obey the gospel of our Lord Jesus Christ. These shall be punished with everlasting destruction from the presence of the Lord and from the glory of His power."

Some have suggested that God must be incapable of this kind of eternal rejection. The truth is that He has not done any of the rejecting. In fact, in the last days, as the ultimate power of God is revealed, some of those who recognize their sin will not ask for mercy—they will instead seek shelter among the rocks and cry out to be hidden from God (Revelation 6:15–16). The state of the human heart in rebellion to the Lord rejects any responsibility for sin. However, there is no excuse before the justice of God because it has rejected the mercy of God as revealed in Jesus Christ.

What Is the Millennium?

The Millennium is referred to in Revelation 20:1–6. It refers to the binding of Satan for 1,000 years (a millennium) as Jesus and His people rule during this time. At the end of this time will come the final disposition of all things on the earth. There is no other direct reference to this in the Bible. Many scriptures have been assigned to this period of time, but there is no direct relationship to this text except by the inference of the interpreter.

Once again, the essential matter concerning this period of time reinforces God's ultimate victory and the partnership of God's people in realizing the coming of His Kingdom. All other observations about the Millennium are sidetracked from the purpose of the prophetic instruction of the book of Revelation—that God's people are victorious over the works of the devil as they remain close to the Lord and continue in prayer in the fullness of the Holy Spirit. Everything else only feeds the imagination.

The "Whens" of
REVELATION

When will the rapture of the Church take place, and when will Jesus return? These two questions are quite possibly the greatest points of interest in all of the prophetic speculations. Jesus answers clearly—"It is not for you to know" (Acts 1:7); "Watch therefore, for you do not know what hour your Lord is coming" (Matthew 24:42); "The Son of Man is coming at an hour when you do not expect Him" (Matthew 24:44).

We do know these things about the coming of the Lord: Jesus Christ will return unexpectedly—"as a thief in the night" (2 Peter 3:10); He will gather His own together at His coming—(Matthew 24:31); when Christ returns, all His people from all time, even the dead, will be taken up with Him (1 Thessalonians 4:16–17); we know that it will happen "in a moment, in the twinkling of an eye" (1 Corinthians 15:52); everyone will see it—"as the lightning comes from the east and flashes to the west" (Matthew 24:27); and no one will miss it—"For the Lord Himself will descend from heaven with a shout, with the voice of an archangel, and with the trumpet of God. And the dead in Christ will rise first. Then we who are alive and remain shall be caught up together with them in the clouds to meet the Lord in the air" (1 Thessalonians 4:16–17).

There is a great deal of controversy in the Church about the details of the return of Christ. Some believe the "rapture" (lit.—"caught up"—1 Thessalonians 4:17) will take place before the return of Christ. Clearly, this passage of scripture suggests they happen simultaneously, as does Matthew 24:30–31. For those who take a literal, chronological view to the book of Revelation, they place the rapture of the Church in Revelation 4:1, before any of the judgments of God or the beginning of the great tribulation period. That theory, of course, demands that the trumpet which is heard in 4:1 is indeed "the last trumpet" according to 1 Corinthians 15:52.

There is no absolute sense in which any of the interpreters can be proven completely certain about the timing of the rapture or the return of Christ. But one thing is as certain as God Himself—Jesus Christ is coming again for His Church and we must be ready!

What Is Our Response?

First, our eschatology (the study of end-times) must bring us to a place of absolute humility. We do not know when—but we do know Who! Jesus is coming again! And He is coming for His own people "who have loved His appearing" (2 Timothy 4:8). Our opinions about personalities, timelines, and events may well fuel interesting speculation, but they offer little instruction into how to structure our lives in anticipation of His coming.

"Therefore, since all these things will be dissolved, what manner of persons ought you to be in holy conduct and godliness, looking for and hastening the coming of the day of God" (2 Peter 3:11–12). Our instructions are clear in the Word of God— "But you be watchful in all things, endure afflictions, do the work of an evangelist, fulfill your ministry" (2 Timothy 4:5).

In character and conduct we are to be blameless; and in our mission and passion for the lost, we are to be diligent in our witness. And we are to be constantly vigilant in our awaiting the Bridegroom's return (Matthew 25:13). The book of Matthew offers the illustration of those who kept their vessels filled with oil (the Holy Spirit) and remained faithful in awaiting His return. Our instructions are clear, and they are not difficult at all. Jesus is waiting to return. It is only God's mercy which restrains His coming for He is "not willing that any should perish but that all should come to repentance" (2 Peter 3:9). In the meantime, our questions about the book of Revelation should be submitted to the broader truths and responsibilities which are clearly outlined for us—let's continue in them until He comes again!

PART 3

PRACTICAL WISDOM FROM REVELATION

JACK HAMILTON

RETURN TO THE DAYS OF
TOMORROW

There is a strange fascination with the future. People long to know what events are out ahead of them that will have an impact on their lives. This urge to know tomorrow is born of inquisitiveness and fear.

It is the inquisitive who seek some inside insight which will give them an edge in controlling their destiny. It is another vain attempt to be godlike. This pursuit of unknown details of acts and events perpetuates the hold the forbidden fruit of Eden has on the human soul (Genesis 2:16–17; 3:1–6).

The emotion which drives this quest is fear. If something disastrous is looming out there, perhaps it can be avoided if prior knowledge is obtained. This imagination is the justification for this search. Fear of the unknown drives people to seek out a means, usually through some occultic practice or practitioner, to inquire about the future. The anxiety about the evil possibilities of the days ahead drives people to desperate activities. These acts of desperation do not bring peace but only multiply fearful thoughts and concerns.

Jesus addressed this pointless pursuit when He said, "Do not worry about tomorrow, for tomorrow will worry about its own things. Sufficient for the day is its own trouble." (Matthew 6:34). Worry and fear over things that have not yet happened is non-sensical, because tomorrow's misfortunes may never happen. And besides, today has enough trouble, temptation, and testing to occupy our attention.

It was the Lord Himself who taught people to pray for two very important graces of God that will manage the fears of the future.

People are to ask for the Father's Kingdom to come (Matthew 6:10), that is, that God's rule and power would superintend the lives and circumstances of those who will believe that He is in control of everything and will care for them.

Jesus also instructed people to cry out for and believe that God would deliver them from evil, including the evil one (Matthew 6:13). This declaration of faith underscores a person's confidence that God's power is available no matter what is being faced or what is yet to come.

Throughout history geo-political, socio-economic, and spiritual-moral dynamics have affected the life of people on the earth. And for the most part this record demonstrates that people have lived under oppressive, brutalizing, and dehumanizing conditions. Is it any wonder that there is faint hope in the human soul for better days ahead? The cry for justice, peace, and security has perpetually echoed from generation to generation. The haunting question is where and when will these historic worldwide conditions be changed.

God has not turned His attention from this human dilemma. He has initiated a plan of redemption for all people, and to understand it one must return to the island of Patmos in the first century A.D. At this site the last of the original apostolic band encounters the Risen Christ. He hears, sees, and writes things that not only apply to him and his peers but to those of future generations too.

To those of us who make up John's tomorrow constituency, there is a message of true hope. Therefore, no matter how tyrannical human regimes are, or how oppressive demonic activities become, the words of Jesus Christ cement the soul in faith and trust, "For the Lord God Omnipotent reigns!" (Revelation 19:6).

No book in the Bible has drawn the attention of people concerned with the days ahead than has the last book of the New Testament. The Book of Revelation was written by the Apostle John at the direction of the Christ. Inspired by the Holy Spirit, the writer describes things yet to be in the context of his present reality. While the prophetic imagery stimulates study, it is the practical counsel and commands that anchor the soul.

God alone knows all things. From His knowledge of historical, contemporary, and future events, He commissions John to record these things. The purpose is to comfort the early Church during its time of witness, exhorting them to faithfulness amidst pressing trials. At the same time, its message unveils the totality of the triumph of Christ over all evil and the consummation of the present age.

The Revelation presents the basis for today's believer in Jesus in maintaining an overcoming lifestyle and solidifying hope for the age to come.

People who get trapped in trying to chronologically interpret its message soon are confused about the signs of the times. Trying to overlay an understanding of today's events on the things that John writes about dilutes the essential communication of God to His Church contained in this report.

The Book of Revelation should not be viewed as a kind of sanctified crystal ball for looking into the future. It is a panorama of how God has orchestrated the overthrow of evil through the work and exaltation of the Lamb of God (Jesus the Christ). One essential element used by the Lord in this thrust of righteousness is the Church. And since this redeemed people are a principal part of this eradication of sin and wickedness, the Holy Spirit inspires John to write what he sees and hears at the command of the Risen, Exalted Christ Jesus.

Christ's objective for this manuscript is subjective interaction with His commands to all believers for all time. Pastor Jack Hayford has written that at the opening of the Book of Revelation Christ calls the faithful to **patience**, **purity**, and **pursuit**.

Each believer is to patiently stand firm in every struggle, for victory is sure. While doing this, they are to live in purity each day motivated by the understanding that Jesus is coming again and soon. With these factors in place, they acknowledge that their true pursuit is the war of faith in every conflict knowing that the real enemies are not flesh and blood and because souls are at stake (Ephesians 6:12–13).

Pastor Hayford continues by writing that the Revelation directs us to: (1) Live in faith while facing personal trials; (2) Live obediently for the shaping of personal character; and (3) Live for evangelism as a personal mission (Pastor Jack Hayford's handout at 1997 Pastors Seminar at The Church On The Way, November 10–13, 1997).

When this document is approached in this manner, there is a lessening of confusion. This happens because people are not trying to identify personalities, develop time lines, or match contemporary events with the recorded visions of John.

John is faithful to communicate that this writing is the Revelation of Jesus Christ. **The information is important.** Therefore the promise is that all who read, hear, and keep the things John writes about will be blessed (1:3).

The Personality is paramount. Jesus is everywhere in this Book. His appearance at the beginning is catalytic. His communiqués to the seven churches are vital for developing the resolve of an overcomer. He is in heaven and on the earth. He is leading the Army of the Righteous and governing a millennial reign. He is comforting the brutalized and judging the wicked. He is creating a new environment and destroying the systems of bondage.

Finally, Jesus assures the trusting believer that He is coming soon. In the last chapter alone He states His intent three times, "I am coming quickly!" (22:7, 12, 20).

The Revelation stimulates the expectation of the faithful, not with deferred hope but with such forthright promise the Spirit and the bride (the Church) say, *Come!* (22:17).

JESUS AND THE CHURCH

The Church is people called to serve the Lord and His purpose. They are called out of the desperate conditions of their world and their own personal calamity (*ekklesia*, from *ek*, out of; and *klesis*, a calling). These are the ones to whom Jesus promised His personal involvement in their development and His superintendency of their activities.

Jesus is identified as the Christ (God's Anointed, the Promised Messiah) in Matthew 16:16. Upon this revelation, He stated that the Church was His personal agenda and that they would be an overcoming people, "I will build My church, and the gates of Hades shall not prevail against it" (Matthew 16:18).

In the Book of Revelation there is an expansion of this theme and confident hope. As far as the individual is concerned, the fundamental call is to live in faithful anticipation of the return of the Lord Jesus (22:7, 12, 20). The believer is constantly reminded throughout this letter that the Savior is returning, and this promise fortifies the personal ability to stand firm even amidst the most threatening of situations. It may appear that evil is winning, but the reality is that because of what is written in the Revelation, the people of God are confident of ultimate victory (13:7–10).

Another aspect of personal exercise is the call of Christ for faithful prayers of intercession tempered with worship that is amplified by praise. Both prayers and praise are consummate acts of worship. And they are directed to "the One Who is worthy, the One slain, the Redeemer, the One Who has made us kings and priests to our God, Who enables us to reign on the earth" (5:8–10). This constancy in intercessory prayer and worship allows for vision beyond the horizon of human experience. It underscores the heavenly reality of the Lamb's worthiness. This prayer experience testifies to the Lamb's authority to alter with righteousness the temporary power of evil.

The principal ways for people to prepare themselves for such fundamental actions are twofold—first, by reading and absorbing into the soul the words of this Holy Writ and receiving the promised blessing of this discipline (1:3); and second, by training the soul to hear the voice of the Spirit of God. Believers have been prepared that the Spirit is speaking expressly (explicitly) in these latter days (1 Timothy 4:1), and the admonishment of Christ to the reader then is, "He who has an ear, let him hear what the Spirit says to the churches" (2:7, 11, 17, 29; 3:6, 13, 22).

On the basis of these fundamental actions, the individual is called to anticipate an eternal destiny of joy with Christ (19:1–10). The hope of glory is real. The purpose of life is not power, influence, or money in this present space/time world. People are called to a higher purpose with Christ. The myopia with which most people view life leads to despair. And this near-sightedness makes the prospect of the future seem meager or hopeless. In the final outcome, however, the Revelation proclaims earthly hope becoming eternal reality for those who are united with the Lamb (19:6–9).

This apocalyptic letter exhorts believers to look to the eternal and not the temporal for the means of processing today's encounters (2 Corinthians 4:17–18). The Revelation makes the calling of each member of the Lord's Church purposeful and powerful, for their destiny is filled with the joy of Christ's eternal presence (20:4–6).

Motivations For Triumphant Living
Encountering the Eternal Christ (1:8)
Embracing Christ's Love (2:4–5)
Enduring Christ's Suffering (2:10)
Embodying Christ's Faithfulness (2:13)
Emphasizing Christ's Works (2:19)
Expecting Christ's Return (3:3)
Enacting Christ's Authority (3:7–8)
Envisioning Christ's Chastisement (3:19)

One thing is dominant throughout Revelation concerning Jesus. It is this reality that makes this Book so Christo-centric.

Jesus is actively present at all times. He is the object of the worship of the Church. He is also active in judging the Church and sustaining it. And it is Jesus who actually leads the Church in overcoming evil, its emissary the devil, and all he represents.

It is the Church (the ones written in the Lamb's Book of Life) that cries out in triumph, "Alleluia! Salvation and glory and honor and power belong to the Lord our God!" (19:1).

JESUS AND THE FINAL CONFLICT
He first appears on earth disguised as a cunning serpent. He really is that fallen angel who is known

in heaven as the dragon, the Devil, and Satan (20:2). This Adversary of humanity is an unrelenting foe. His manipulation of people and ironfisted abuse of them is seen throughout history.

This enemy has developed a world system that withholds human dignity, oppresses with poverty, and murders innocents on the one hand. On the other hand, he appeals to human pride, moral weakness and lusts of all types which condition people for blasphemous living.

Satan's strategies against people can be reduced to his manipulation through fear and lies. As the one "who deceives the whole world" (12:9), he is the malignant personality of human history.

Jesus witnessed his fall from heaven *like lightening* (Luke 10:18), and defeated his attempts to compromise Christ's integrity through the schemes of evil temptations (Luke 4:1–13).

A clear aspect of the purpose of the coming of Christ, the Son of God, was "that He might destroy the works of the devil" (1 John 3:8). The decisive defeat of Satan is in the Cross where as *the ruler of this world* he is both cast down and judged (John 12:31; 16:11). However, in spite of having his power broken, the Devil is relentless in his scouring the earth "seeking whom he may devour" (1 Peter 5:8). Satan's hellish wrath intensifies "because he knows that he has a short time" (12:12), and he deploys his demonic hosts to torment and control all people.

The redeemed of the Lord may feel the Devil's heavy hand, but they are equipped to overcome his assaults. Having been arrayed in the armor of God, they are able to quench the fiery darts of hell (Ephesians 6:13–17). It is also "by the blood of the Lamb and by the word of their testimony, and they did not love their lives to the death" (12:11) that frustrates the encroachment of the evil one."

It is in the Book of Revelation that one can see the finality and conclusive judgment of God against Satan, the systems of his evil domination, and all who are held under his control (20:7–10). The Lamb who was worthy breaks the seals of the scroll (5:9) and now sits on the throne where there is no more curse forever (22:3).

A. Triumph Initiated by Worship (19:1–10)
  1. The worship of the heavenly multitude (vv. 1–3)
  2. The worship of the twenty-four elders and four living creatures (v. 4)
  3. The worship of the Church (vv. 6–9)
  4. The worship of John (v. 10).
B. Triumph Through the Incomparable Warrior (19:11–21).
  1. The Warrior's appearance (vv. 11–16)
  2. The Warrior's affect (vv. 17–21).
C. Triumph Over All Evil (20:1–15)
  1. Evil bound (vv. 1–3)
  2. Evil silent and righteousness rewarded (vv. 4–6)
  3. Evil eradicated (vv. 6–15)
D. Triumph Originating a New Environment (21:1–22:5)
  1. A new cosmos (21:1–8)
  2. A new dwelling place (21:9–27)
  3. A new reality (22:1–5)

JESUS AND ISRAEL

God's covenant with Abraham has never been revoked. While Gentiles have become akin to Abraham through faith in Christ, they have not replaced Israel in the scope of the promise. God's redemptive plan has always included Israel's faithful remnant. The prophets of God (Isaiah, Ezekiel, Daniel, et al.) have spoken and encouraged Israel to repent and open their hearts to the Messianic Kingdom personified in the Messiah Himself.

In his characteristic way of asking rhetorical questions, the Apostle Paul inquires of his readers in the Book of Romans, *Has God cast away His people?* He then answers his own inquiry, *Certainly not!* (Romans 11:1). The cultivated olive tree (Romans 11:23–24) is the promise of God to Abraham, and branches of a wild olive tree (Gentiles) have been grafted in. The natural branches (Jews) will be grafted into their own olive tree again as they are embraced by faith in the Hope of the Ages (Jesus the Messiah).

In Revelation 7:1–8, the faithful care of the Godhead for Israel as a people unfolds. In the midst of the initial judgments of God, He sends forth His angel *having the seal of the living God* (v. 2) identifying the faithful of Israel. This action directed by God is reminiscent of that which is recorded by Ezekiel where a divine messenger with stylus in hand was to go through Jerusalem of that day and put a mark upon the foreheads of those who hated the idolatry that filled the city. Those who were marked were the true servants of God in contrast to those who polluted the testimony of the Lord

(Ezekiel 9:4–7). The marked ones were saved from the impending righteous judgment of God.

The sealing language of Revelation 7 has the effect of assuring the people of God of His concern and plan for them. As the trouble on the earth increases these of Israel who are sealed are spared from the wrath to come.

The Revelation continues with a description of the measuring of the temple of God (11:1–2), and the assignment of the two witnesses implies that God is continuing to deal with Israel. His plan is to enfold them into the community of Christ as they are acknowledged at the heavenly rebuilt temple. There is a fuller work to be defined, but Israel's hope is linked with the Lamb of Revelation as they stand with Him on Mount Zion *having His Father's name written on their foreheads* (14:1–5). They are singing a new song and stand without fault before the throne of God.

A. The Seal of Israel's Position (7:1–8)
B. The Seal of Israel's Place of Worship (11:1–4)
C. The Seal of Israel's Promise (14:1–5)

JESUS AND PURIFICATION

When the Lamb begins to unseal the scroll, what is revealed is an understanding of how the people of the earth have been tormented because of the way in which the forces of hell have had their way. Everything and everybody has felt the devastating effects of the horrible hate of the Devil. The seals are the tale of the visible Church in a violent world.

The seventh seal releases the sounding of the

seven trumpets of judgment. These terrible activities are to bring the people of the earth face to face with the consequences of their resistance to God. The fifth and sixth of these trumpets are woes of overture. The first of these woes is the hateful torment of demonic beings released from the abyss, who afflict people indiscriminately. The second woe is an irresistible horde who kill without pity.

Despite the awfulness of the depictions of these two woes, the people of the earth continue in their idolatry and immorality without sorrow. Their hardness of heart and harsh activities set them up for the third woe and seventh trumpet.

With the sounding of the seventh trumpet, the bowls of the wrath of God are poured out on the earth. It is the worst of times but end with the best of times.

These judgments of God are not for punishment. They are intended for the purification from sin. They effect the riddance of evil from the cosmos. God's creation and creatures now experience the pristine nature of their beginnings. While John's portrayal of this time is unimaginable, it nonetheless leaves a righteous impression on the soul who reads the account and solicits the exclamation—

Even so, come, Lord Jesus!
(Revelation 22:20)

BIBLE BOOK-A-MONTH STUDIES

The formulation of the ***Bible Book-A-Month*** concept was born in the heart of Dr. Jack Hayford to help people achieve three things: *systematic*, *substantial*, and *thorough* coverage of the Bible.

The Triangular Approach

There are many worthwhile approaches to a study of the Holy Bible—for example, "synthetic" study—which draws together highlights to provide a quick grasp of a book; "critical" study—which assesses the ancient textual resources that authenticate the trustworthiness of the book as a document; or "verse-by-verse" study—which seeks to exhaust every book of the totality of its content.

Distinct from any of these, the ***Bible Book-A-Month*** study seeks to achieve the maximum possible grasp of a book's truth, while keeping a pace forward which sustains the average Bible student's interest. It is <u>demanding</u> enough in its *academics* to seriously engage those interested in intelligent, thought-provoking study. Yet it is <u>dynamic</u> enough in its *movement* to avoid losing passion and to keep each student at a point of continuous anticipation.

This is done through use of a **"triangular**

approach" to each book—which focuses the three primary things to be found in every book of the Bible.

1. Each Bible book contains an *essential message*: the core concepts which distinguish that book and provide its place in God's Word.
2. Each Bible book presents *problems* and evokes *questions.* Good Bible study helps questioners find *satisfactory answers* to reasoned inquiry, even as it demonstrates the *relevancy* of God's Word and discovers the power of the Holy Spirit revealed in each book.
3. Each Bible book provides *practical wisdom* and *personal guidance*. In each book, *insights for faithful, fruitful pathways* will show how to adopt, adapt, and apply the Bible to your life, as Jesus' disciple.

Triple Tools—Support Resources
1. Each study is accented by a *pocket-sized book* as the one you have in hand.
2. Pastor Hayford is in the process of reading the whole Bible in the New King James Version on audio cassette. These can be ordered in conjunction with the *Bible Book-A-Month* program.
3. Overview teachings of each book are available on audio cassette as recorded live at The Church On The Way.

Additional resources, noted in each volume, can be ordered by calling Living Way Ministries at 818-779-8480 or 800-776-8180.

BIBLE BOOK-A-MONTH STUDY RESOURCES

STUDY PAK

The <u>Study Pak</u> on Revelation includes this book and two tapes by Pastor Hayford. (One tape is an overview of this study, and the second tape features Pastor Jack reading the entire book of Revelation.)

SPREV $12

STUDY ALBUM

The <u>Study Album</u> includes this 72-page printed overview of Revelation along with three audio teachings by Drs. Hayford, Bauer, and Hamilton with an additional BONUS tape.   **BBAM09 $15**

*Call 1-800-776-8180 for information
on other Bible Book-A-Month studies!*

WHEN WILL THE CHURCH GO UP?

This series discusses whether the Church will experience a pre-tribulation rapture; the things we do and do not know about our Lord's return; and that His return for His Church is a clear and faithful promise to believers. It includes a discussion of God's assignment to believers to watch and occupy until the Lord's return, and a study of Daniel 7 with the biblical answers to the question "Will the Church Escape Persecution?" (4 tapes) **SC011 $19**

UNLOCKING REVELATION

Explore THE BOOK OF REVELATION with Jack Hayford in these ten audio tapes. Dr. Hayford teaches verse by verse and precept upon precept in this dynamic expositional series. The ten tapes come in an attractive vinyl album complete with study notes. **SC438 $48**

Teachings that transform—

DEMANDING QUESTIONS ABOUT CHRIST'S COMING

This series encourages believers toward an attitude of expectancy about Jesus' return, balanced by a practical determination to "do business" until He comes. Pastor Jack Hayford discusses topics such as "Will You Be Ready?" "What Are the Signs of Christ's Coming?" and "What Will Happen When Jesus Comes?" (6 tapes)

Audio **SC069 $30**
Video **DQCVS $36**

The following videotapes are available in VHS format: $12 plus shipping and handling

The Year Jesus Comes V3237
Preparing an Ark V3240
Waiting Out the Last Days V3738
Tuned to the Trumpet series:
       When Jesus Comes V3862
       Accountable to His Word V3864

The Spirit-Filled Life Bible
"the resource you can trust!"

The
SPIRIT-FILLED LIFE BIBLE

The Spirit-Filled Life Bible is a powerful resource for enriching your relationship with Jesus Christ. Faith-filled, prophetic, and Spirit-empowered insights are featured in this one-of-a-kind study Bible. Here, in the light of God's Word, you will discover a Spirit-filled life rich in godly characteristics. English or Spanish.

Hardback Library Edition
reg. $37.99 **SFLHB $27.99**
Burgundy Genuine Leather *reg. $74.99* **SFLBG $54.99**
Black Genuine Leather *reg. $74.99* **SFLBK $54.99**

SPIRIT-FILLED LIFE BIBLE FOR STUDENTS

This New King James Version resource for students offers real-life, down-to-earth insight for living the Christian life in today's world. It has hundreds of helpful annotations, maps, charts, and articles on major Bible themes.

Softcover **SFLBS $15.99**

Unveil the Keys to Scripture!

HAYFORD'S BIBLE HANDBOOK

Hayford's Bible Handbook is an unparalleled resource that uniquely unveils the keys to Scripture, providing not only a wealth of information, but also a spiritual stimulus that will encourage your faith and service to Christ.

It unlocks Scripture with:

- Illuminating surveys of each book of the Bible.
- Helpful illustrations, time lines, maps, and charts; plus an up-to-date discussion of archaeological discoveries that illustrate and verify bible accounts.
- A complete Visual Survey of the Bible.
- An Encyclopedic Dictionary with over 1,300 entries that address subjects of particular interest to Spirit-filled believers.

reg. $26.99 **HBH $22.99**

This guide opens the riches of Scripture to deepen your life in Christ.

DATE DUE

Method of Payment: ❏ Check or Money Order ❏ Visa ❏ MC

_____/ _____-_____-_____-_____ / _____
Signature   Card Number   Exp. Date

14820 Sherman Way, Van Nuys, CA 91405-2233

Please call for prices and ordering information:
1-800-776-8180 • 1-818-779-8480

Please include your remittance (U.S. currency only) with order.
Make check or money order payable to Living Way Ministries.